Buddhas & Angels at the Dump

Buddhas & Angels at the Dump

Cody Owen

Printed in the United States of America

Photographs © by Cody Owen

Shotola-Schiewe, Cody O., 1992-
Portland, Or

ISBN: 978-0-692-82013-1

Buddhas and Angels at the Dump

For my mothers, who gave me the world
For my fathers, who took none of it away

And for you, when I'm "gone", keep going!

(Lento)

And so they woke to broke mothers and depressed fathers who had watched the dumps fill and spill past their traditional demarcations. The cities were tied to the oceans in slime, and growing in piles. Even those that could get a leg up were waiting in traffic for a better tomorrow. We were told of holy separateness, of propertied-freedoms and the globalized market clock, but there was little meaning to be found in hollow commodities. We questioned how idols of individuality could be made of reincarnated parts; questioned the alienation of value from our human, the extraction from our land, and the ignorance of flows. Was there any sacredness in separating the impure from the pure? And what is this method that makes madness of the poor? We were sold the soul, and found only a hole —but didn't know where else to go. Society said, "This, not that" but we couldn't tell the systems from the trash.

Our profit motivated society cultivates sociopathic behavior as we are driven through the throws of the identity cult and its commercial appendages to compete remorselessly inside of our cooperative civilization —convinced of our (pseudo) individuality. These poems are intended to engage like Zen riddles and good news, to point at the cracks in our abstract social constructions and look towards the ground-real unity of myriad beings: the *process* in the *person*. To be human is truly to be empty (adaptable, potential, open) to a changing environment and the next breath. This inseparability of subject and environment enlightens us to the understanding that in the same way a war may make a soldier, a loving father gives rise to a loving son. We have been taught in the black and white illusions, "Human as separate" and "Human as selfish" which are used to legitimate the horded distribution of wealth and power in our global society. These are but flickering forms of the *delusional dualism* that alienates us from our real (material-spiritual) world and each other, propping up a false separation with our constructed human concepts of "self" and "other". When we cultivate this dissonance, it grows like a cancer in the body of the earth —in our minds.

When we focus on surface-level differences, instead of our fundamental sameness, the resilient natural variations we see appear as unlimited and tireless enemies.

While our social experience is miseducated by this ideological (nonreal) dichotomy of Self – Other propagated by the ethical villains of liberalism, we are mistakenly digging ourselves into an isolation of dogmatism. In a world constructed by worded thoughts and fixed expectations, dynamic beings struggle towards openness, togetherness, presence and activation in the moment at hand. Unwittingly, we trap ourselves in a dualistic universe with this fundamental separation logic, where the one-dimensional binaries of Mind – Body, Spiritual – Material, Individual – Group, Pure – Impure, Good – Evil, and Life – Death reign over our perceptions. While these concepts are (practically speaking) useful models, we must know that they are superficial, and that these perceived binaries are truly unities of emergent and dependently co-arising aspects. Pulling this ideological keystone is central to building "new" realistic, reflexive and holistic global cultures (read: recycling growth-production obsessed culture into one informed by the balancing interdependence of natural and socio-energetic systems). This is the miracle of seeing with young eyes, a world in which science and spirituality, or individual-interested and group-interested behavior, are not understood as mutually exclusive but mutually co-arising.

As we toe the brink of ecosystems collapse, global droughts, biblical storms, oil crises and mass extinction, it becomes the natural path for the living mind of the world body (You!), to shuck this *delusional dualism*, and the unnecessary conflict and suffering that arise from our self-flagellating worship of separateness. It is only by seeing to the root of our being —its ever changing reality, adaptive creativity, beautiful similarity and resilient fragility— that we can continue to flourish in this universe.

If we embrace each other in open faith —(to let go of dogmatics like metaphysical and ethical dualism), that our ephemeral individual experiences have an unending, fundamental sameness, we can resist a temporary economic model which would have us compete for plastic scraps, trained blind and separate despite our socially arising production, information and communication revolutions —life may continue to explore itself on this sunny dynamo.

Despite living in an era of animal/human abundance never seen before (as the old material problem of production efficiency has been replaced by the abstract market problems of overproduction, financial excess and lack of circulation in the real economy, characterized by unsustainable extraction and the volatile cycles of growth and collapse) this hypercompetitive narrative of self-against-other is used to drive a wedge between nations, classes, peoples, and is happy to declare that Earth (truly our mind-body-bloodstream) is a resource dump to consume, until we find a new planet. Yet, we must realize, this is the only body-home we will know, and we must be one-ly of it.

Recent scientific paradigm and ancient spiritual paradigm illustrate the co-arising, inter-dependence of the subject *within* the environment, and the invisible patterns between our living bodies, the soil, and stars. We cannot continue to entertain the illusion that we are separate from the ecosystem resource cycles of Superorganism Earth, and structure our global society on this false economic conception which is calculated based on assumptions of short term energy flows, externalities, collecting interest on printed debts, and the eroding separation of the dumps, jails and the metropolis. The Greek roots of our words show us the humanness of our *Economy*: the "household management system" that has been raised up as the false idol *God, the Modern Word and Invisible Hand of the Market.*

A house divided cannot stand, whether we call our house law an economy or an ecology. It has become ethical and existential necessity to cooperate across superficial identities, to compost non-cyclical economics with mistaken waste logics that do not consider the interdependence of ourselves and our socio(eco)nomic house-law systems, which will surely glut and bust the bloodstream of the mind. Our global society is no more than a co-experience and co-construction of ourselves, a continuous spectrum between the hegemonies of structures externalized from the human mind, down to the sensitive micro-cosmic agent with its foot on the accelerator, who must look towards what we might call a *Process Understanding* in respect to our relevant, practical, workable universe.

Look past delusional dualism's false separation of the self and the other, the spirit and the body, the human and the world, and towards our common struggles.

After all, these are
Just a bunch of human words about
Something that cannot be described
You'll die if you take them too seriously

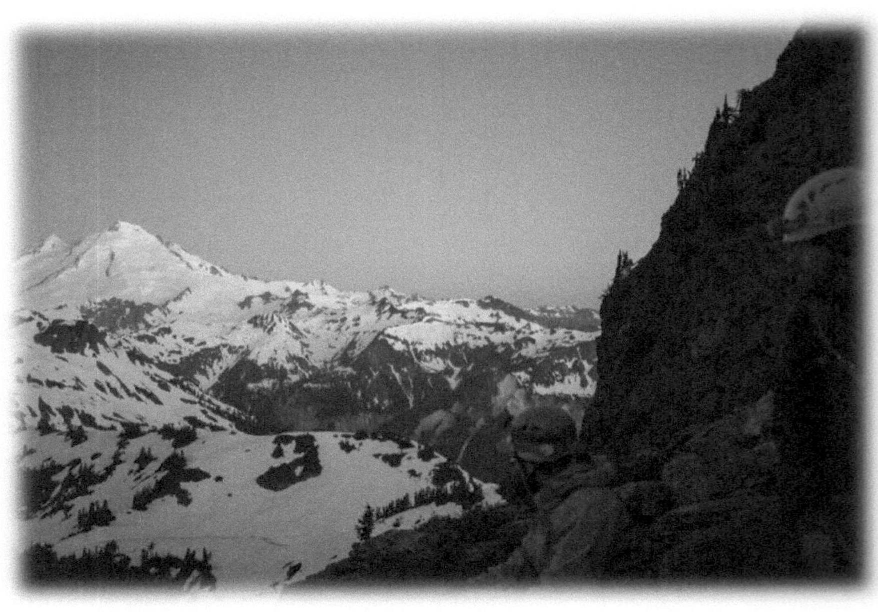

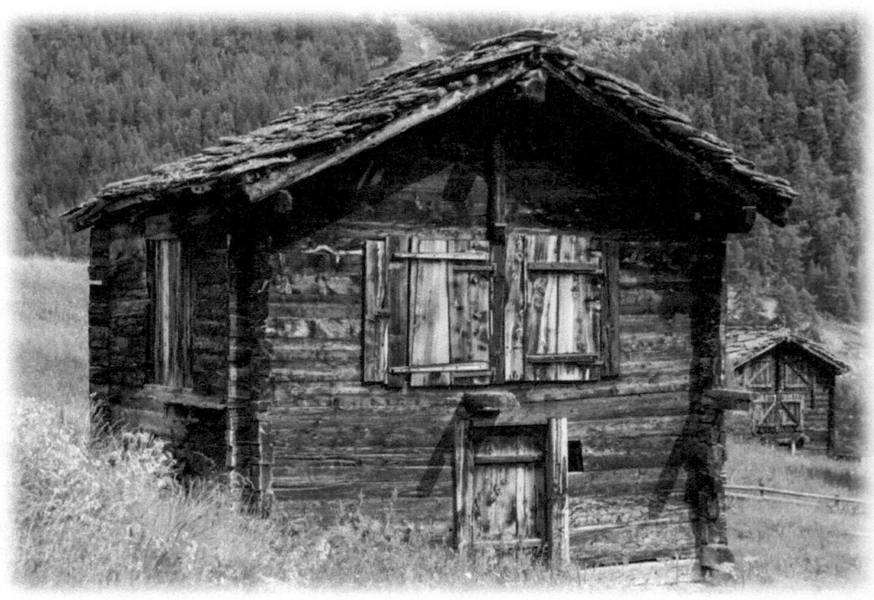

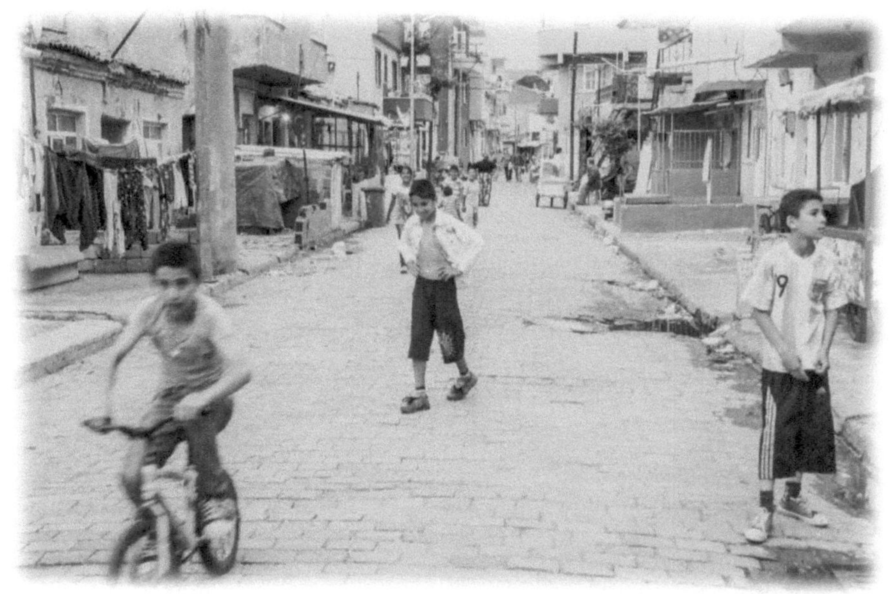

Human Now

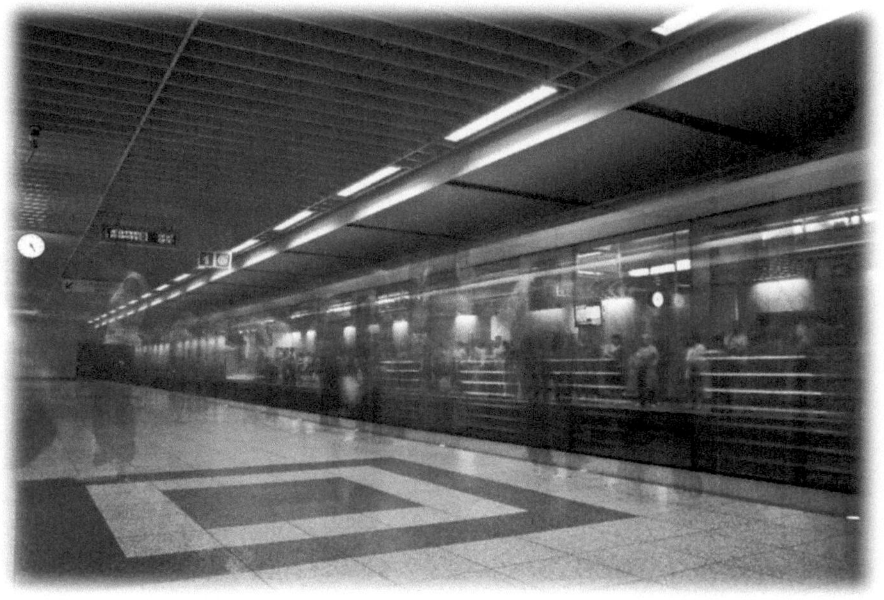

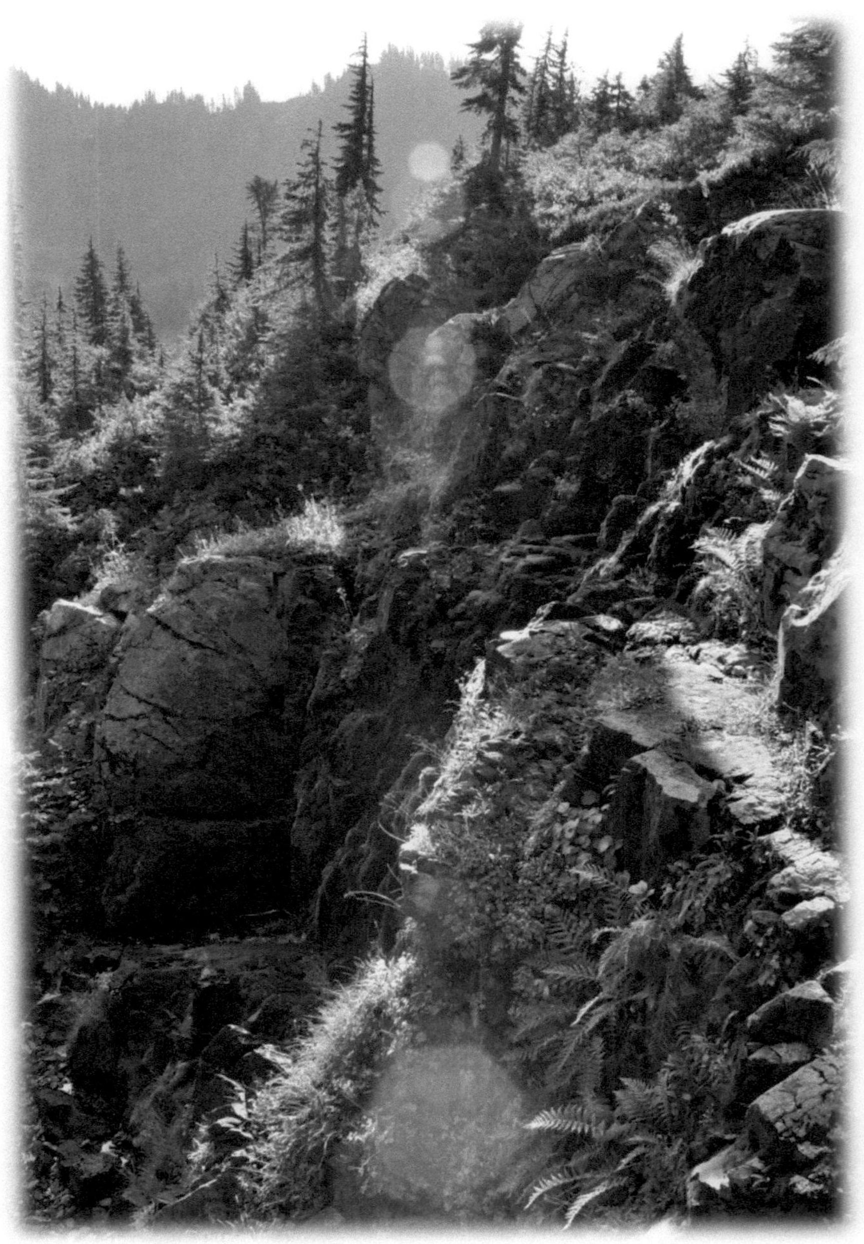

Unending Love

I saw you
And you made me feel
All the way to the bottom of the well
    And when I lost you
I looked for you in the rain
In all the faces that came
There was that feeling, the same

I looked for you in puddles
And spoke to you in smiles
    You kept coming back, sure as spring
So I'd even see you in sand,
In flashes of light,
In the middle of the night
There you were again
The whole time

The House in the Winter

All of our memories like fevers
Genetic intuitions and fears, passed down from dust
Creaky porches and lovely wives
In last night's dream

Be strong in your weakness,
Sure in your impermanence 'cause
You've gotta look at the bottom of the world
Before you can raise it on up

Basement rafters creeping mold and
The corners are full of boxes that
No one has looked in for years,
Stacked boxes in front of these boxes like
Past marriages

The old structures can't save us from this winter
Our families are splintered
We thought love gave up on us a long time ago,
So many loose ends they became a knot of
Nerves sparking in corners

But after living in this constant state of change
For life, we've adapted
Seen the cracks between childhood and maturity
Been them, and tried
Making order out of piles of mud

Ideas that only hold under one house
Whose father inevitably leaves

These winters have left sweet pine needles and pitch
In our sweaty matted hair
Dirt worked into the wood, finish worked off
With a pulse —and our skin,
Calloused so it meets perfectly the place that it has worn

We've given up trying to own anything
        My body in this house,
But I'm just a steward and a mote of dust
Drifting out the back door

So come on up to the house!
There's plenty of room,
You'll help keep us warm
        Besides, we're all dug in so
We might as well hold on till you make it

What I'm trying to say is,
If you're burning up or frozen out, if you're hungry
If you're all strung out and hopeless
If you've got nowhere else to go
Join us!

We need everyone to keep up this house

Manifesto of the Humble Climber

We climb because arbitrary point
To reacquaint self with suffering
Deep eyed wanderers
Questioning leviathan massifs

How many woodpecker scalps do I need?
To alter my economic status markedly?

We climb because we are children of the land
Our specialized bodies go quickly, unused
If we were not to climb it would be sacrilege
Our natural path is dynamic and uncertain
It is the challenge that seduces us

We climb to get high,
To forget ourselves for epochs
    Standing in instant
We have heard the liberated winds,
Sewn the sun ridges with trembling fingers

This is our pilgrimage to the hidden and seeking
To the sound of the frost that is creeping

We climb to feel our connections
Humans are soft things to break
    Monkey minds racing in the valleys and villes
But once broken
Our hearts are left open

We may pass through jeweled sanctums
Yet in the end we are wasted, and we know it

We climb because our bodies are melting glaciers
Our blood the plasma of future stars
Hanging on a dragon's tail with an umbilical cord
We are chopping at abstract formations,
Remembering what has been buried in the sky

That we are a part of it all

The Continuum

Everything would be fine if I didn't have to sleep
Time is gone
I lost it long ago
I buried it in my sandbox
But the box rotted
And the sand spilled into the world

In 10 years where will I be?
In 10,000 who will I be?
When we try to collect everything
We never really touch anything

Diamond Spackled World

Follow human skinned laughing
Up the mossy forest path
Little pine saplings bowing
Here and there in their droplet regalia

River of dusk-wood hair
Color of beatific soil
Chinook salmon dancing through
Rain slicked muscle
Springing in weaving steps, sound of breath
Ground-story of radical humanness

That even after years of rain
There is still a spark
An ancient smoldering

My own soggy shoes
Wearing down roman stones
Coming to the end of men
Old twisting paths

Bending trees with no notions
Slimy slugs with no notions
Tragic me tripping over all my notions

But beneath the stream
Star pebbles twinkle mysteries
    The axe cut steps on a log bridge
Where the river pools
Soft living lips tingling
Rain running down noses
Mixing with kisses at the corners of mouths

Steeped pine tree tea
Bears munching and lumbering about
Diamond spackled world
Joy of singing mist

Pitch the tent on an Olympic bluff
God-seat of the soggy, merciful heart
Dusk spilling wine on our sleeping bags
Breathing in the miracle between laughs
Hornet stings like
Squashed huckleberries on bare legs

Weighing Memories

There is no logic
To weigh memories
Essence of past consciousness
A splash in the electric storm

I couldn't be anyone else
And it's all because of you
You gave me more than I knew I needed
I'll keep saying thank you until I forget to

I want you to remember so badly
    Do you?
It was like weed smoke and wet dreams
I bet the security guards wonder where we went

I was angry at your world, angry at mine
But you just needed a hungover breakfast
And a poor maggot who'd been writhing
Smashed your soft brain with metal and alcohol

Can you still remember what matters?
Can I?

You saw your father's body lain
Down for the last time in the cold world
I gave up looking for god

But you are the same angel force of beauty
    I knew smiling in the dark
A real angel with the strength of your scars
How could you have survived?
Utterly human in that hospital bed
Twisted and wrecked,
Like you tried to kiss a black hole

But you kicked its ass and came back singing
So blinding was your moment I was shocked from the past
        We were lost after so much
But we were lost together

You don't know someone till you've struggled together
Everything else is bullshit accessories and high fructose corn syrup

Grime on the Grimoire

Chaos mind's been twitching all day
Bumping back and forth
Wishing for great inter-human powwow
Wishing for tiny solitude
Wishing for great and mortal ideas
       Missing it

Daisy barks, needs to go out
Takes me by surprise
Giving me a vacuum for quantum peace breath

Rain slicked rhododendrons
Flashing in the street lamp
Clearing the sepulcher
So there is no one babbling in my head

No minding the pine needles,
Soil she brings in
       Take it all,
The grime on the grimoire

All the secrets revealed by letting a
Dirty old black lab
Sleep with you in the clean bed

Moon shimmers still
Untainted in muddy wheel ruts

Ode to the Microcosm

Perfect little knot
Doing your dirty job holding the whole non-one,
Inseparable, annihilated carbon-diamond net

Swirling and coiling in waves of space
Made by the meeting
    Binding, composing
All in itself
Of what it isn't

In relations, spiraling outwards-inwards
Mind star in the milk stain subjective
Body spot at dusk in the falling sea surf

Mutually-arising space and point
Quivering like a planetary body in imaginary time

Thanks for keeping it together
Yours,
The Macrocosm

The Black Cat

Hume St, Portland

Pokes his head
Through my door
Wearing a tiered mask of shade slats

Green eyes
Meet brown eyes
My legs crossed

Rhythm with curious nose
Void-space twitching

But I am not food
Not yet

Today I Woke Up a Raindrop

Precipitant of
        Nirvana dream cloud
Falling from matrix mother
Opportunity/womb

This new state seems cold, individual

But in my realization I am not alone
                      Not separate
As I begin to fall
        I mix
        And reflect

More
    Than I
      Can count

Below me,
Innumerable drops
             Falling before

          Around me,
Innumerable drops being born
      Opening eyes in their quivering dawns

Above me,
Innumerable drops waiting to
Take form
           Ready to poke heads into space

All of us driven in the same way by unexplainable force
At once inside and outside, in
Appearance of peopling directions
Which can be only known beyond words or names

Fireflies trail the vein of molten light
Burning to dissolution as they fall through time
God head drinking-pissing process
The water bodies falling-flying

Falling out of all, back into one
Through drenched time
Getting caught in the dust

Rolling
Splashing
Breaking our form in the stone
        Like eyes,
Whetted and carved out of water-light

Hisses of sundering lives
        The path of I
The drop
Appears to end

Until a laughing being drinks from a laughing stream

The Names of Dead Men
Somewhere in Oregon

You wander like a Zen planet at night
Down the wise crumbling volcano
Up the universal highway

Big bang vessels workin'
Screamin' heavy songs
In your torn ear drum

Just a bag of flesh
Casting shadows in the mental peripheries
Of dozing drivers
       Wonder
If you were there at all?

Formed stone weathers, frictioned paths
Rubberfeet souls kiss oil sheen, nonattached
Rushing world's tattered plastic and
Discarded corn husks

Don't need a grandiose ride,
Just follow the purring tail
Lookin' for a place to sleep
Distant trees preach peace

Hop up to the overpass
Take a look around, past the ivy
Shrug off the weight
Lay down in the dust

Honest country boys park their trucks to see
If you're ready to die?
Buddhas in the night with halogen halos
Coming with questions for your squirming bag of sweaty dreams

Eyes speak with sun
Time to scramble on
Before the brain gets too hot
Chomp an apple and   breathe
        Heel rolls to toe
Bits of mountains in your boots
Bits of boots in your mountains

Silent world
Rushing world
No one knows who you are

Mantra

Give it away
Give it away
You never had it

Give it away
Give it away
You always had it

Give it away
You can't keep it
Give it away

Into the Human Moment

Lizzie knows the bouncer at the nightclub
Points to each of us, to me
"Him too"

Into Dante's Sunday night
Into the crumbling brick city-mind
I wonder about all the pairs of dirty feet
That have walked through here
        Wonder if there was ever any dirt at all
Or was it just the idea of dirt in my mind?

Go-go girls crawling like the bodies of gods
Before we burn them

They're breath is covered in beautiful flesh
Dancing on the column of fetish civilization
In their moment, enjoying it in spite of the judgements
Brutal cultures of the pit, the things people might say
All of us enjoying it too, as we get our momentary look at the play

This hungry marrow youth vessel,
Body twinge in the loin of unification
Separated parts and the reconciliation of filth and perfection
Forgetting our preconceptions and
Sharing the human moment

Dear Jack,

Of all the writers I miss you the most
Like the way I feel lame
Because I'll never read all the books in the library or
Be in love with everyone at once and forever
     It's the most beautiful madness

People may know you as black and white
As drunken night
But I know you as Be... and Why?
Pointing between the East and the West

I know you like a harmless beer my dad swigged
When I was a little shitinthewoods,
Drawonthewalls chaos child (as if not anymore)
     That was before I knew any goddamned words,
Just playing out in sticky summers
Empty bottles clanking out spontaneous Zen mantras

Saying to me like your delirious footsteps
You can't fall off the Matterhorn!
You can only fall up the mountain,
Can't ever step off the road
Or escape the dharma kisses the stars blow

Jack, I forgive you for your historical misogyny
     Maybe no one told you
They crushed the Mill Girl's strike in Lowell
A hundred years before you were born

Is it that you saw my déjà vu?
A vision of us eating steaks drowned in violent wine
Our knives shining like cream colored horses
In the sweating pestilence of jungle cities
Or was it your nightmare of what America would become?

My dear Jack,
I miss you like you had fixed dimensions
So I'll visit your grave in my mind
    Staring in the mirror
Watching the dying words in our dancing eyes

Crooked River Karetaki
Smith Rock, Oregon

Smear the toe
In the immaculate pastel morning, renewing
Lucid dreams of golden stone pantheons
Hanging in the sky

It's a miracle how you can stand
Without much of a nick on the rock
Here you are tied to the cosmic rope
Kick back, feel the stretch

Sage brush washbasin looks far away like
People look through tiny portals,
In the past or off in some other valley
Like it was forever ago

But it's not
It's right now!
    Just like you, meeting
Dewy moss and bloody finger tips
Breathing the wordless prayer of wind
Into which you dissolve and recompose

Look for a spot to put your foot
Place with intentionality
Follow secret routes all through the fixity

Where is there to go but here?
Who is there to hear but you?

Sit, Will you Share with Us?

Leaves everfall
Evergrow
Golden dances of the ground
They don't sound when you're not around

The sky is made of whalebones
Crushed to powder under the mountains
    Brought out in wooden bowls for feasts
And we discern shapes
In the bone mist

We of the myriad hearts
Our pulse sounds familiar
    Listen
Can you hear us?

We of the myriad variations of bodies
Our vessels hewn of gravity, condensed light
    Reach
Can you feel us?

Our tables laid of oxygen
Of hydrogen oscillation
And raunchy carbon intercourse
    Sit
Will you share with us?

Breathe Bloodbody, Breathe

Rise bloodbody
Open your eyes

Murmur to the stars
Bloodbody, marvell at the sounds
Eat things off the ground

Curl your fingers bloodbody
Squirm in your dripping dawn
Learn the words bloodbody
Sing along

Chomp the snowball
Bloodbody rake the waves
Remember the things you forgot
Put your dick away!

Get it together bloodbody
See the vessel in the eye
Twinkle like a raindrop
Before you die

Rise again bloodbody
It's all new
Suck the wine from the rock
See your truth

Cut and sew the cloth
Bloodbody raise your totem
Feel the tingle of the unbroken

See the scene bloodbody
Get your peace
See the people for their feet
    Reconcile science, wisdom, mysticism
Bloodbody, it's all we've got and
There are diamonds to be scavenged from this rot

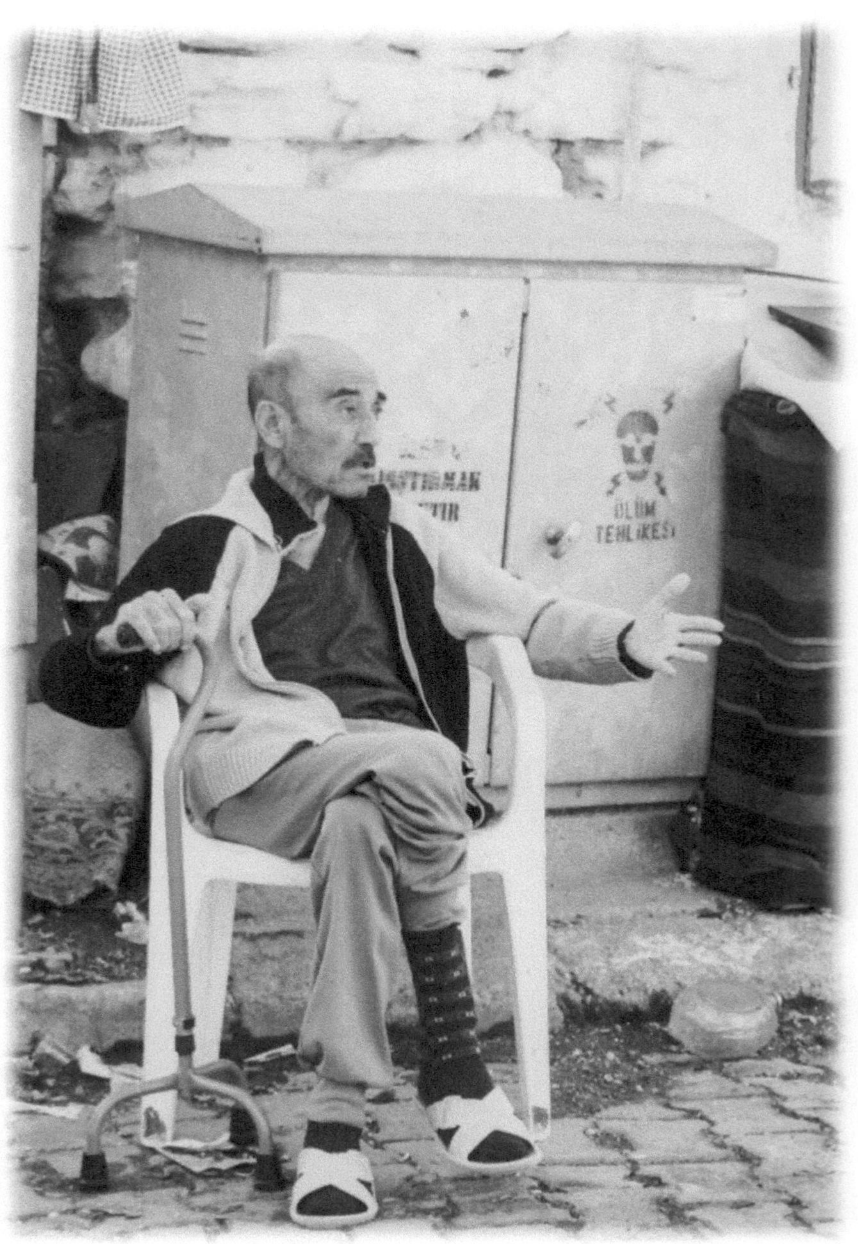
ÖLÜM
TEHLİKESİ

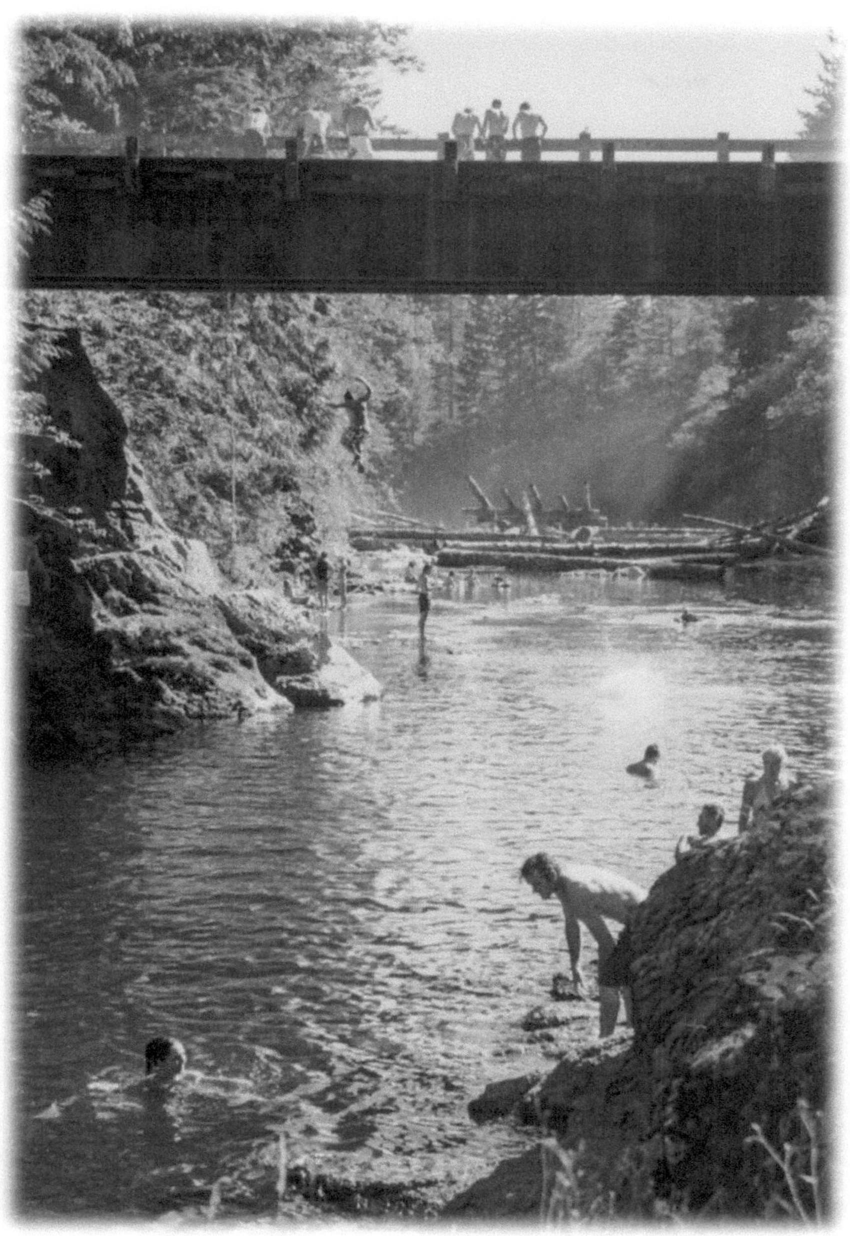

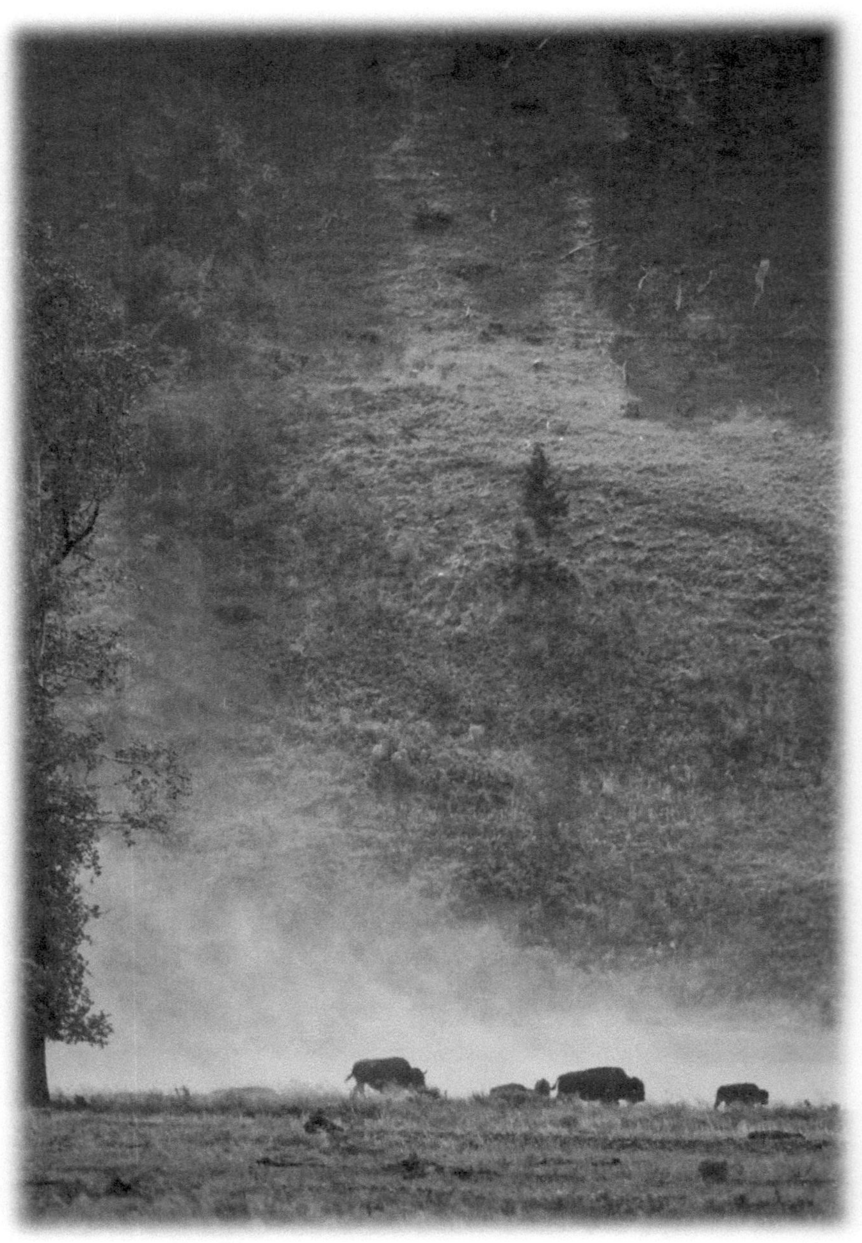

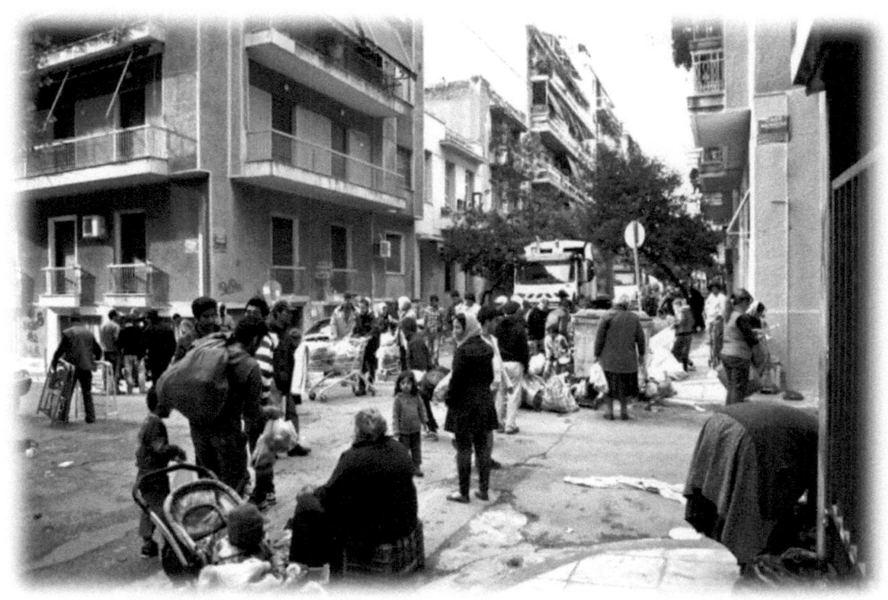

Buddhas and Angels at the Dump

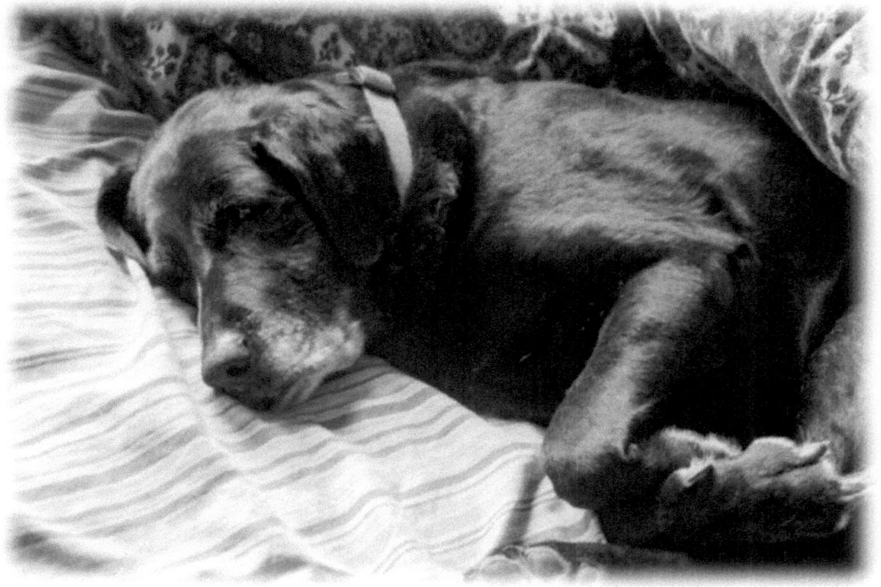

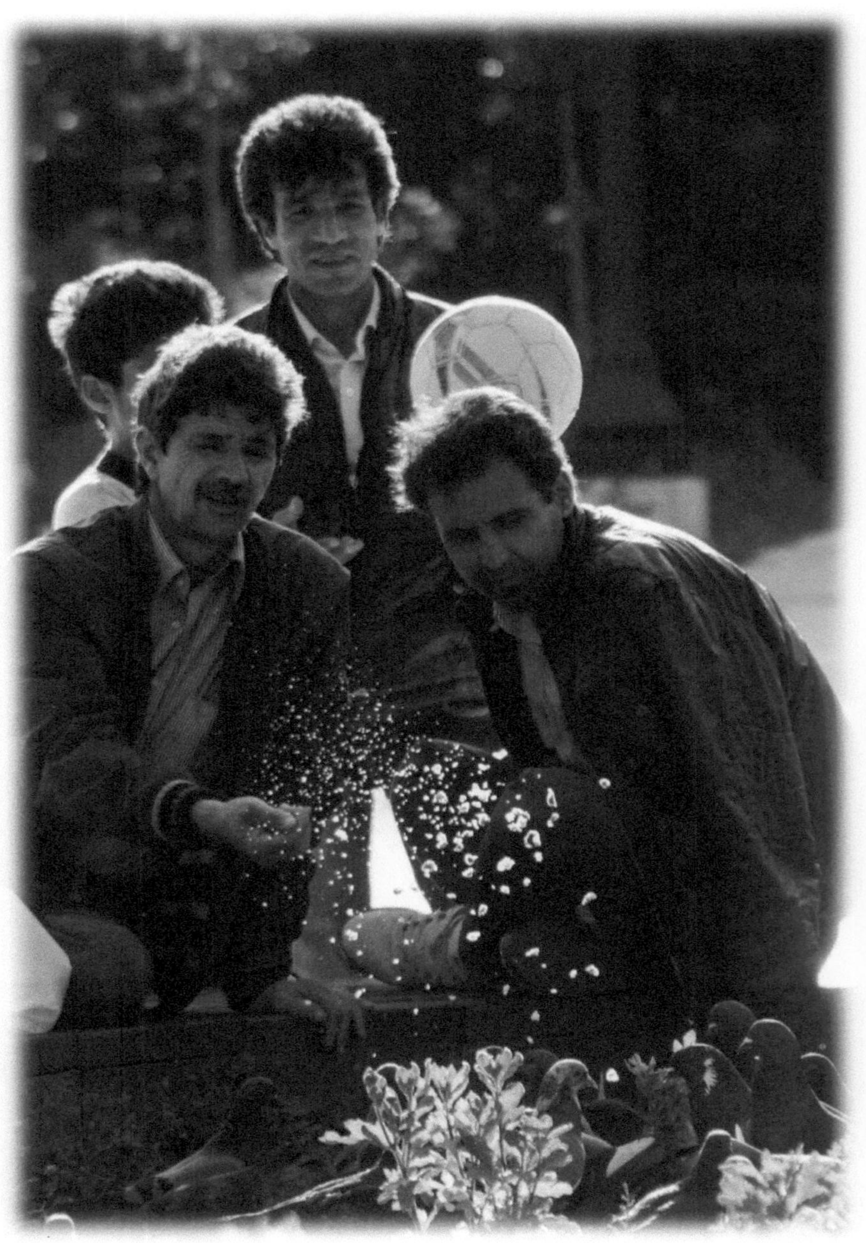

Lost Angels
Bellingham, Washington

You can see angels everywhere
In their floating, temporary bodies
Angels of wandering confusion
Angels of suffering life

Angels born in the dumps of cosmetic industry
(But there's no difference between body and divinity)

Perfectly imperfect human form
Fettered by preconception
Wings drowned in dark blood
Tortured muses intoxicated by human wine

Can you see them?
Screaming for a father out of reach
They hang their heads in the squares
What can you say to stop the tears?

Can you see them?
Dragging ethereal smoke
Burning to feel past the mundane
On amber streets where shadows are infinitely deep

Can you see them?
Staring into campfires amid cold woods
The pain of their sisters reflected in shimmering lakes of hope
Beloved wrists shaking, scarring

I love you all
All who face the bile of life
Embrace that you are lost
That you are on the righteous, muddy
Path that only you can make

Transcend fires of good and evil,
Perfect and ruined
Desire and renunciation
Heaven and the Fallen world
     It has all fallen out

You are the true saviors of humanity
Seraphs twisted, sculpted in the wisdom of life
May you reconcile all of the pain with the truth

Angels who are wonderfully lost
Let us all be lost together
     We only have so long to be lost
Take solace in this

Breathe in this carcinogenic air
And sing gloriously through a haze of incestual ideas
Deconstruct, wander, stumble, learn, and forget
Let yourself be happy tonight

The morning is ever blooming

Church Made of Mud

Yamhill, Oregon

Follow the rain
To the end of the country road
Winding like a mind between pools of light
Towards holy shining windows in the night

Headlights of caked-on oil boxes
Threaten to jump like wildfire, off the road and
Into the next property

They too, pass like a frog splash
Out of the corner of your eye, into wet grass
Turning up the rutted drive
A shovel stands gleaming, ready against a tree

Come into the warmth now!
There's an open bottle of wine waiting at the bar
Sit down and give your souls a rest!
Pass the peace pipe and rave, so
Heaven can hear the musical lives

Out in a pasture somewhere
We burn the last oil lamps
In a glass house covered in lace

If you can forget all that nonsense outside this moment
     You can remember that
God doesn't care that you tracked mud in the church
For Christs'sake
The church is made of mud
So paint your face with it and take up the sword

To Have a Dancing Heart

Bumping, blending bodies
Lost in the who's who
World a reflection of vacuum selves, efficiencies unfulfilling
Humming futuristic lullabies

Tension building in the backcountry subconscious
Spindrift from the cranium couloirs
Building cornices ready to break
    The ice is speeding up

A deficit of now cannot be dealt with later!
Do not decline a dance
Though the music may be industrial,
May seem artificial

A dance of despair
Will equally work kindness
Like sticky resin
Into your wooden, knotted heart

So if there is a whorling dance to be had
And there is
We must let our hearts limber
So they can bow and spring back
Like orgasmic laughing trees

Hotels and Souls

Vancouver, B.C.

All of us squirming and boiling over
Becoming billowing clouds of gas
Buying and selling pieces of phantom like Allen
At our beat mother's funerals

Drinking and fighting and crawling
In and out of beds like Charlie
On our father's front lawns
Our stories strewn about like scars on our faces

Morality worlds where the wars are a course of routine
Heavy coal smoke and trading beds between shifts, living
Spike festered Orwellian halfie-lives
Serving dystopic meals labeled "gourmet"
From basements where it is easy to hear the boot stomping

All of us praying for the elevator to heaven
    We picture our grand hotels differently
Cloud Nines and Flamingos built in spiritual deserts
Trying to get above the plastic Mickey Mouse lobbies
Built on prisons that echo bound souls
Langston dredging damned rivers with his human psalms

The housekeeper Pindy
Leaves us mints made from her tears
Which we will only taste for a few moments
While we visit this room

Visiting all the other souls
Who have cried, laughed, loved, dreamt
In this bed
Ate naked lunches and couldn't sleep in this bed

Scratched, hollered, watched, fucked in this bed
All of us tossing and turning and waking and dying
In this bed of bone and blood and good clean dirt
Covering our flailing bodies in floral patterns

But we can't tell who's been who
After the maid has visited
Who asks under her breath
  "Where did the soul come from and where is it going?"
The maid who will never travel to exotic hotels
She is waged to beat the skin out of our skin with her skin

She signs her name on the housekeepers note,
It says:
  "The angels are buried in filth"

Allen Temple Church - Police Brutality Protest
King Neighborhood, Portland

Wake up world!
Wake up!
My brothers are dyin'
My sisters are dyin'

Strike the orthodoxies of domination!
Neighborhood church sinking in waves of gentrification
Blood sticky, sweaty-sweet struggle seats
In the house of revolutionary Jesus

Good gaunt pastor who saw the maw of hell
The history of black boys
Strung up in American oak trees
Cocks cut off
Shoved in their mouths

Some disenfranchised black Christ
Crucified every night
Shot in the modern street, told to lay down easy
    How are you gonna be free without any property place to be?
Locked in the modern jails
Taking the modern wage

Are you free yet?
Wake up world!
Wake up!
My brothers are dyin'
My sisters are dyin'

You could read the list of all the names
But it's easier to count the raindrops
"Post-slavery" police bullets
Falling on the capital-fracked neighborhoods

Auto-Rational Cannibal

Man got caught in his own meat grinder
Best way to make energy, make work, make profit
Is to grind down the bones
Of the dumb, hopeless poor

Feed on the rent of the debt
    Kings and slaves in newer clothes
The dismembered hands making flat screens, searching
Through burning metals,
Festering lungs, brains driven to psychosis
Man trained in terror, surplus extracted

Private propertied fear of Other... Self?
Didn't realize all he had to do was look inside
See the plague of fear he cultivated
Flourishing like rot in the mindless heart

Addicted to possession (or did he get lost looking for love?)
Convinced himself he was a genetic machine
Worshipped his evil, fed it as such
    Then he beat it into his sons

Mystified by self-alienation
Pressing technocratic buttons
Never enough?
Auto-rational cannibal process: growth at all costs
Better for who? Better for why?
Better for human social ecosystem?

Cooperative animal in denial
Pretends illusions of separateness,
Dissonance with radical social emotion,
Root connections of material systems
    Seeking fulfilment, finding cheap power

Dominate spirituality with man-god idea
Dominate nature with self-down hierarchy
In short centeredness crush glaciers, paradise forests which lent us
Our lungs —made into ice cubes and drugs

Put up shopping centers instead
Breathe wealth, spit everything else out
Confused flows, growing of their own
In spite of nations: Federal Reserve to IMF to Hong Kong
Capital turns faces, melted, churned
All the cosmic-comrade mammals burned

Smiling like a cold Rolex
As the Alps melt
G.I. Joe won't buy shoes made in China
But Vietnam is alright

Tricked himself into the
Facade of States –the most organized gangsters
Over the people to be chewed
Spit out, when there is no more muscle to use

Rationally build the best bomb
Rationally revert to fundamental meaning amid the meaningless
Rationally legitimate American, African, Global eradication
Explain that you must have done something wrong to get raped
That you're from a backwards place
That you deserved this

Don't ask "why?" you nonconformist
Why are we living?
Why are we driven
To eat our own to nourish the Self?

Drop the cold stones
Wash your face in the river
Off come the human germs
See the body for the storms
Conglomerated into water structures
Freeze-thaw mountains murmur, rush
Buildings, and their civilizations crumble
Calm frosted paths to mystic roiling chaos

Swarming molecules boiling out of molds
Buds bursting contradictions
Ganges to blue jeans, glaciers to power structures
Creative destructions and inevitable revolutions

Middle Way

Everyone needs their space
Even the Soviets didn't share pants
Sure, maybe they'd offered to buy the Levi's off your ass
But now even the Levi's are made in Vietnam
And Ford has a plant in Thailand
And women can work in the exploitative free trade zones
So broke Americans can still buy clothes they slap a designer label on
As if this was a true emancipation

We took Communism to the barren gulag,
Capitalism to the wasted dump

Cultures of work and cultures of money
Run around till the world is ragged
When there's really nothing to do
But make your warm sanctuary and
Lay down calmly

I Put the Space Under Floating Mountain
M.L.K. Blvd., Seattle

In some past life
I put the space under floating mountain
    Or was it this life?
I don't remember

"The" space in the engine
Leaking into the non-engine space
Notions and compartments
    Floating mountain is leaking into floating space
In my mind

Car is broken?
I checked the engine — it was still there
    The wheels are always turning anyway
Bodhisattva mechanics with greasy hands
Making sure of this
Working with laughter and patience

First generation immigrant families
    Authentically American
Driving to work in duct taped cars
Stopping for hurried McRituals

Next to the mechanics shop
The rickety house is a mosque
    Flaking paint, wires frayed
Cars crammed around
Some post-modern performance of the cosmic Kaaba

Church lot down the street
    Grey, torpid body
Cars speed past throwing pieces of the void
I tell myself "No trash, no church"

Forgive them all, my small self too
        Limber up the body again

Rusted metal temple fence
Plastic Buddha statues and cinder blocks
        Pacing the concrete garden
I bow to the simultaneous ignorance and wisdom of flesh
Of metal boxes that hold explosions
Of bodies that hold notions

Water the grass
Cut the foot off a rabbit
Hang it in your sports car
        But I can hear the flayed beings
Meat-factory civilization that reeks like Auschwitz
Eat everything that's dumber, feebler than you till
You're chewing your own feet

We all put the space under floating mountain
So I'll be sitting in the corner
Eating simply and praying through the din of WWE Divas
Hitting each other with chairs

Cat in a New Jungle
Hume St, Portland

Little black kitty
Green sickle eyes
Cancer in his paw

Cocks his nebulous ear
Listens to the sounds with his mind
Scanning for an unwary sparrow
      Whole forest decomposing, recomposing
Hungering and feeding itself in nourishing cycles

He knows the crooks of the roots
Learned the tendencies of the leaves
Bark bits, creak of the warped door
With a fast body to explore the wood
But we're getting mangy

A yang spot
In his Yin fur
Seed of change under his claw
So more cats can come

Cats for whom
This will be a new jungle

Don't Worry
Planet Earth

You've got it together
It's all going to be fine
It's all going to be fine
Keep it together
Don't worry
    We'll be dead soon
All of us will be dead soon.

Don't call me a pessimist!
I'm trying to comfort you!

If you don't like what I have to say
    Don't worry
I'll be dead soon

Aren't you glad?
You don't have to drag that ol' body around forever
    The river keeps washing up new shells
Manifestation made of variety and contrast
No difference between forms and their happening

This is the ultimate human struggle
The anxiety of time-death
And the fingers becoming sand
Birthing prophets and beat poets
Our fear of the darkness

But can't you see it's useless to resist?
Beyond the desire to persist
Don't worry
We'll all be dead soon

I am doomed and you are damned beautiful
Especially your worn, calloused feet
You make dying look like living
And we are your curious witnesses

All of us will be dead soon
Don't call me a cynic
I'm trying to comfort you

Aren't you glad to see?
The human will never conquer death
No matter how many slimy cities we build
No matter how many beasts we devour
Or oceans we drown in trash
Humans will never conquer death

We like to build sandcastles

Dream the Big Dream

On Sunday morning we shook off the ashes
Blew on the embers still burning underneath

I didn't know what I'd find at the end of the road
Burned brighter because of it
So I opened up quick and bawled Diamond, dripping oil
Into the sated yawning god mouth of the Columbia
Secret misted ridges and great still rivers
All things meeting in heaven's instant

Jack played songs which rambled on, and had brought the boys
Home from the jungle
I drove like Dean, pushing on and on
Without fear of death or call of sleep, coasting down the passes
Feeling the calm explosions under my toes

There was still light in the sky when we reached Montana
And I saw the land stand up out of time like the golden rule, or the
Funeral mounds of numberless Indians
Imagined trying to get the first train over those
"Damn, me!" Rocky Mountains before winter, and
     Realized
There was still something worth standing up for
That the backbone of the Americas wasn't apes driving go-carts
Over a world of golf-courses

It was getting the brothers and sisters together
Before the end of summer;
And besides, if you're going to dream
Why not dream the Big Dream?

Moving Towards Togetherness

Now Daisy follows me around the house like
She's afraid to die alone

But who can remember all the walks we've had?
After all, we'll go on walking after our bodies go limp

We all want to be held on our way, as we go
    Out in the garden of love, with a steady hand
To be sure that we were there, with our eyes
Showing each other our tender emptiness

Some days you just want to wash it and start over

But what if we forgave the selves and their anxieties?
    To see the blooming in the breaking

I loved you, after all

Diamond Webs

The faces fall
Like smoky raindrops
On the edge of the wood
Flashing from the sky
Rolling back to the sea

Pop! And up we sprout again from the ground
Fairy rings of sapling Nows
        Heaving, glowing in rinsed mist
Blood Ink, fresh from the worldbody
Splattering ratty tapestries, writing our treatises

The rabbit nose twitches on a log in the lock
Ferns bite into the sky, they are hanging
For a while into space, like mountain earth-teeth
Totality doing in same way: Seeking and Hiding

Rock islands receding into icy echoes
Up they grow until they reach your nose
Then   *Sneeze*
They're gone

Trees shrug like laughing monks
Happy with the trickle of sun on their silly brooms
The nonsensical braille wisdoms of bark and
Spiders hammocked in their windy beds

Shining points in diamond webs

Shattered Mirrors

Sleeping in post-Vietnam, shell shocked in Mid-East
Somebody's son
Capital war machine's done with 'em
Criminalized for having no place to go
Break their mirrors in frustration

Mother's crying degeneration
Depression, debt and divorce
Taken out with the trash
Don't get a cent for their labors
Nursing all the new beings

Shattered mirrors
Wrought in the diamond mines
We dance on the caverns buried in power
        Silenced histories of dripping tears
Assembled consumption line compartmentalizing
Hides relationship between slaves and devils,
Underdeveloped and development

Flowing out of Africa, South America, rural Asia
Through the sterile suburbs
Gentrified blocks
Used and discarded
Shattered mirrors end up at the dump
Sill cracking smiles somehow

Newborn into burning reality
Could be spotless, could be numb
Just needed time to be young

Bodies wash up on the shore
Next to tattered bins from fukushima,
Slime-bay messages of energy's emptiness
Adorned with plastic bag halos

What industrial muck
From which to grow
Sure lets strong lotus!
While automatics clatter
        Boys to bullets
Leash still on the sacred vagina
They sell rape like plastic, shiny bodies and
We bought it all
Trained ourselves to be gratified instantly

If you're not careful
There will be poets and philosophers
Brawling in the street with monks and Christians
While the bankers watch on pay per view

Among the molding piles of formed concepts
We may go rotten, let the dust collect on the mirror
        Forgetting the present corroded bell
Ringin' like a bent bedspring, with the truth of temporality

Watery ecosystems slippin' on the oil slick
Storms over the sea planet
Offshore capital rigged
System to exploit the coral eyed children
What's gonna be left?

Flickering shadows stand in
Craters of traditional value systems
Externalized waste piles, families scattered
Burning in the alienated distance
Leaving concrete rubble and smoke signals in annihilated space

But we're not communicating with these annihilated meanings
With this imbalanced language of wealth
Where the mass of them read but can't write, think but can't speak

        We have no control, and our edges dissolve
Like notions of imperfections, dogmas we forgot
Death, failure, hierarchy – they forgot us
Windshield wipers go shlick shlack
Acid raindrops swept... away?

Down the drain?
Where did you go?
I only know myself in relation, though
All fountains of blood flow from the same source

Desperate bodies blinking for love
Alignment of parallel quasar kids
Smiling like blooming lotus'
Amongst all the confusion, ignorance
Structures of fabricated violence
Which inevitably decompose
The way rust grows

Don't you see the faces in the slime?
Just crazed babes in the sleet and the mud
See the mirrors through the grime
So angels may rise up from the dump

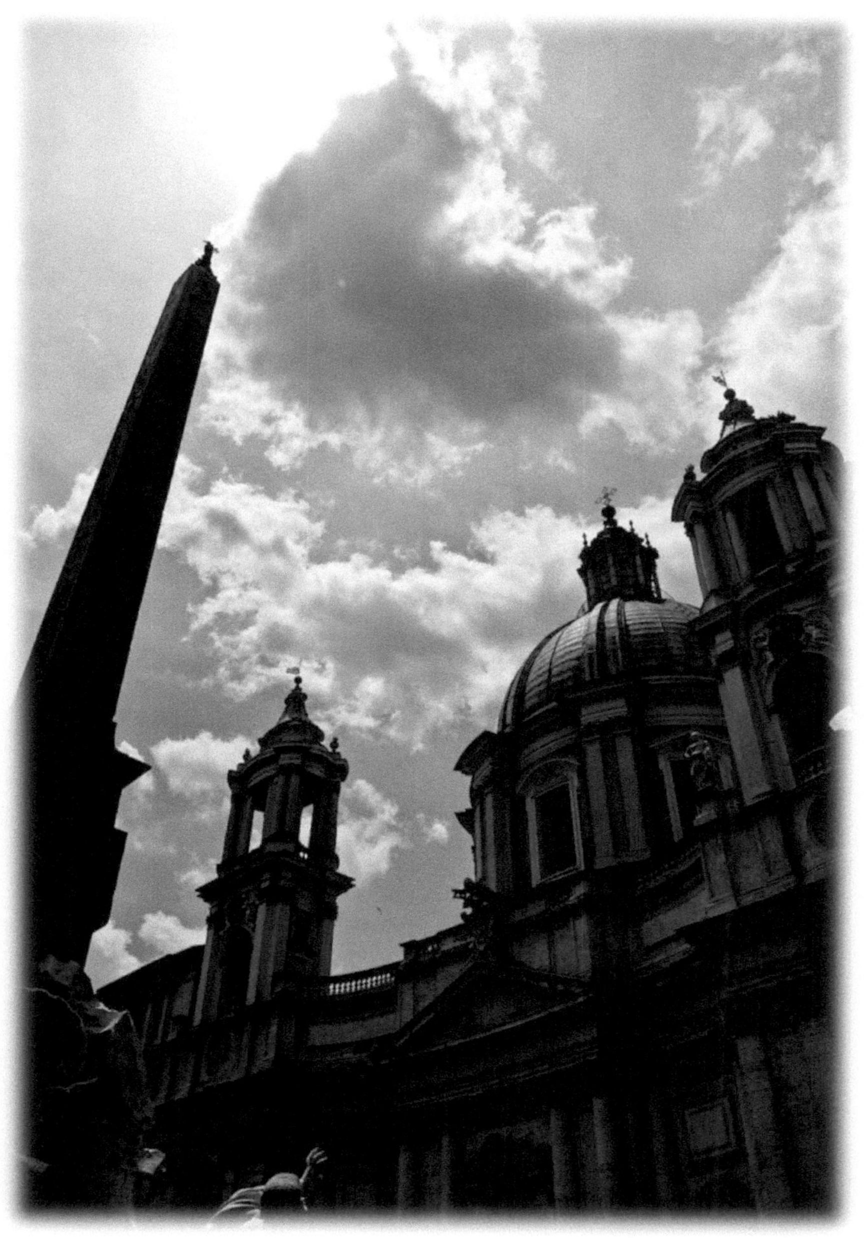

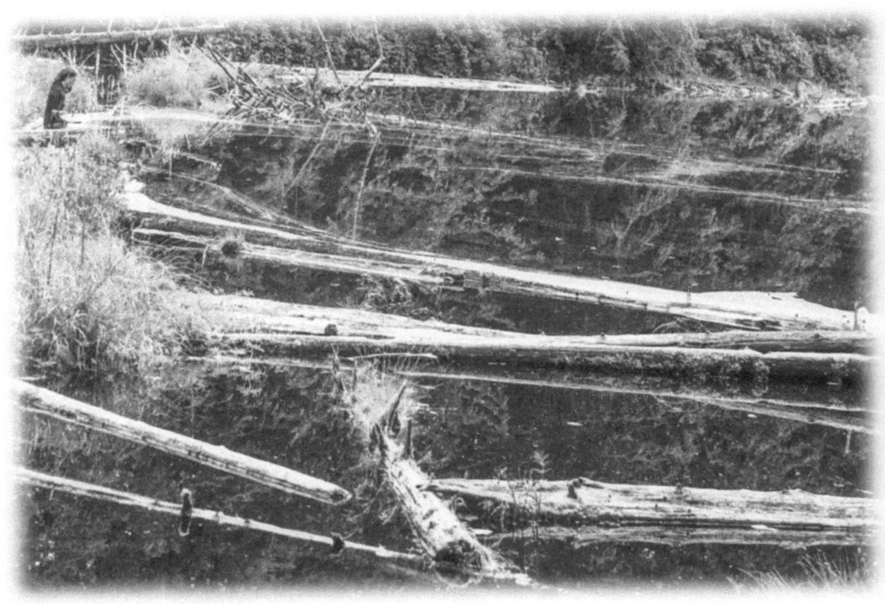

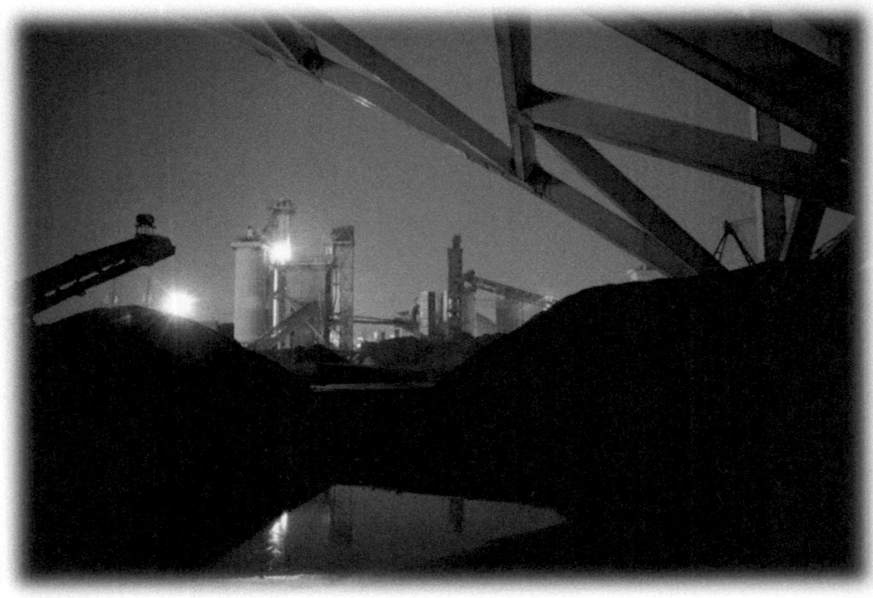

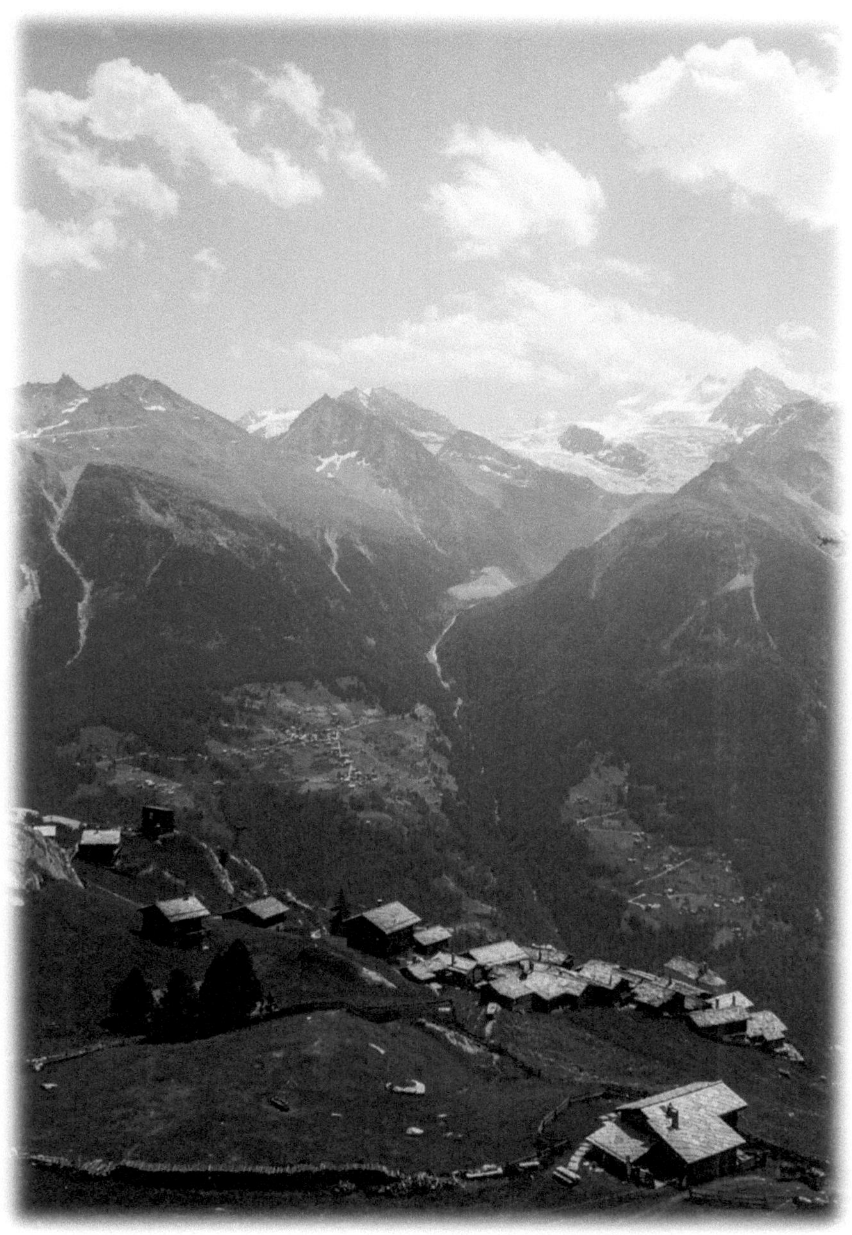

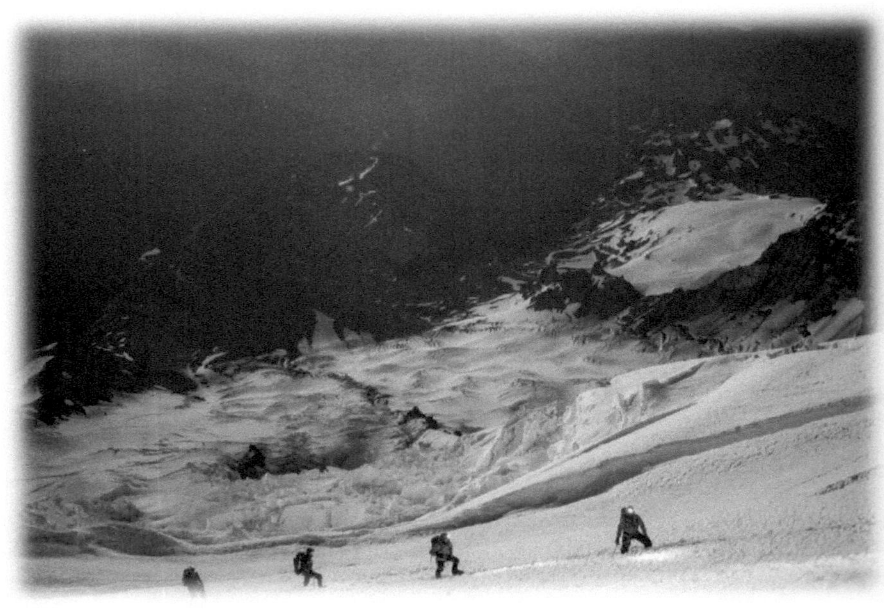

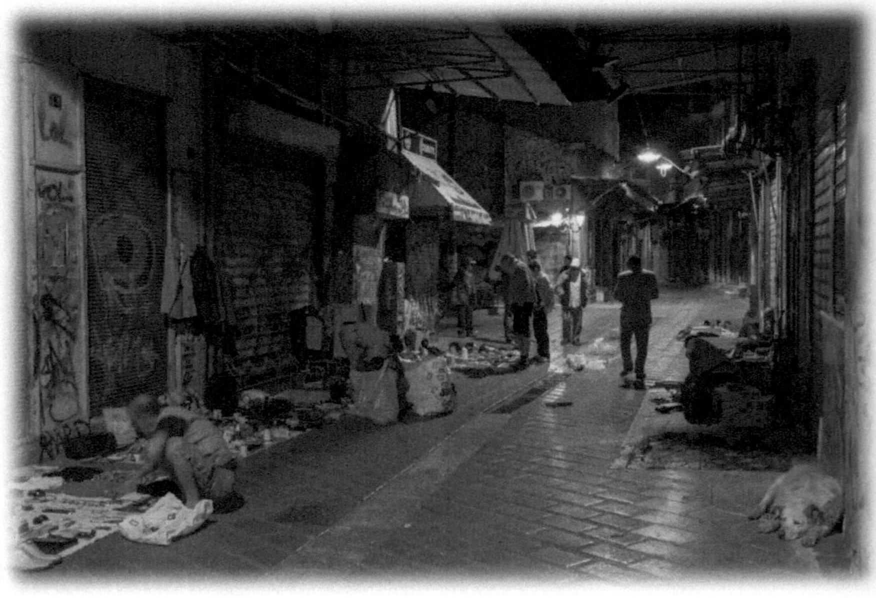

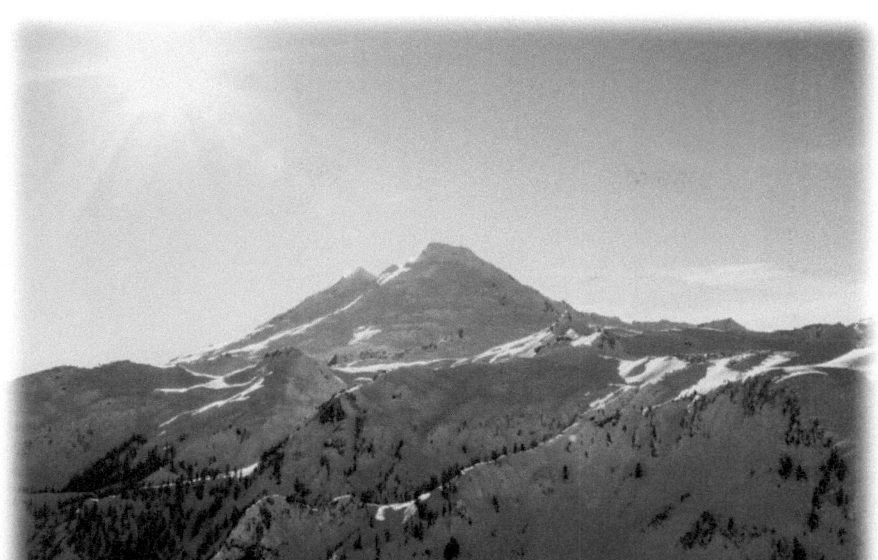

Overflow

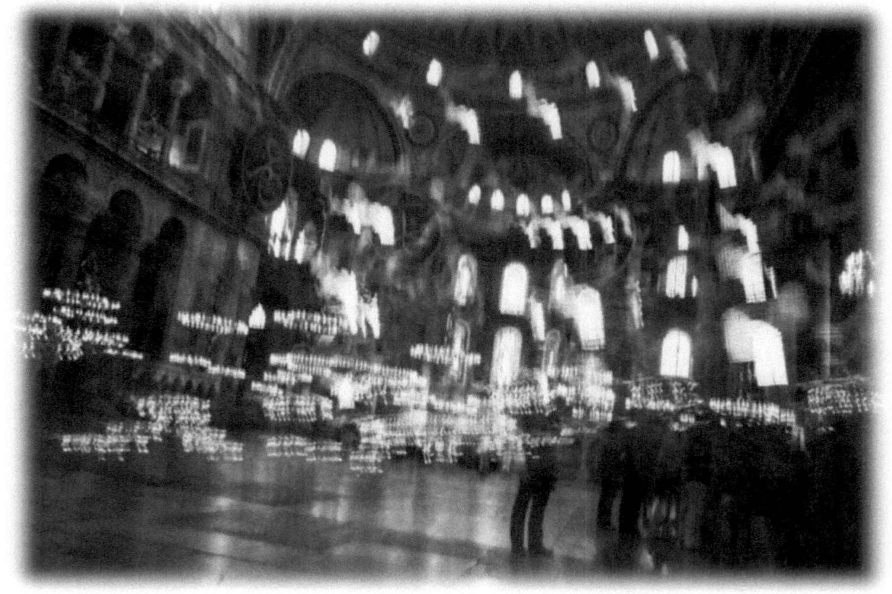

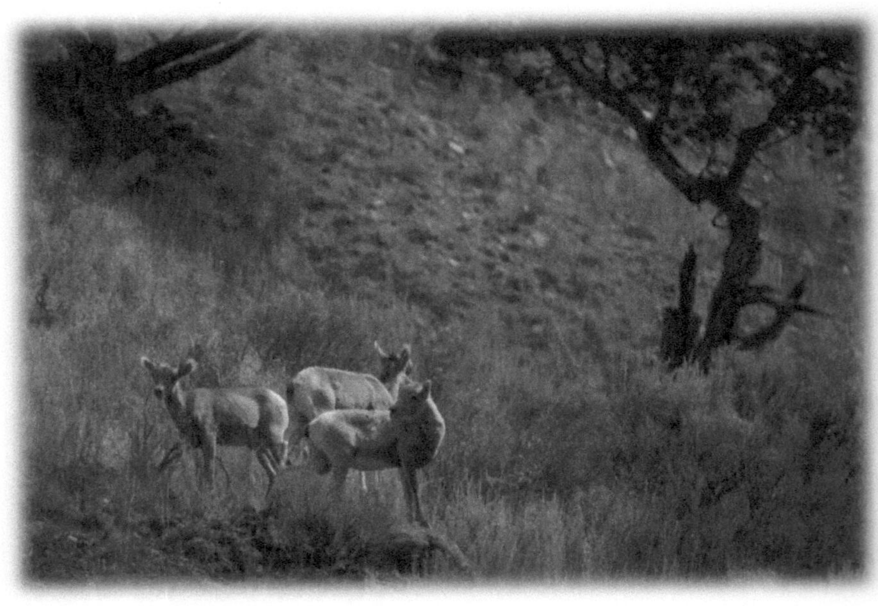

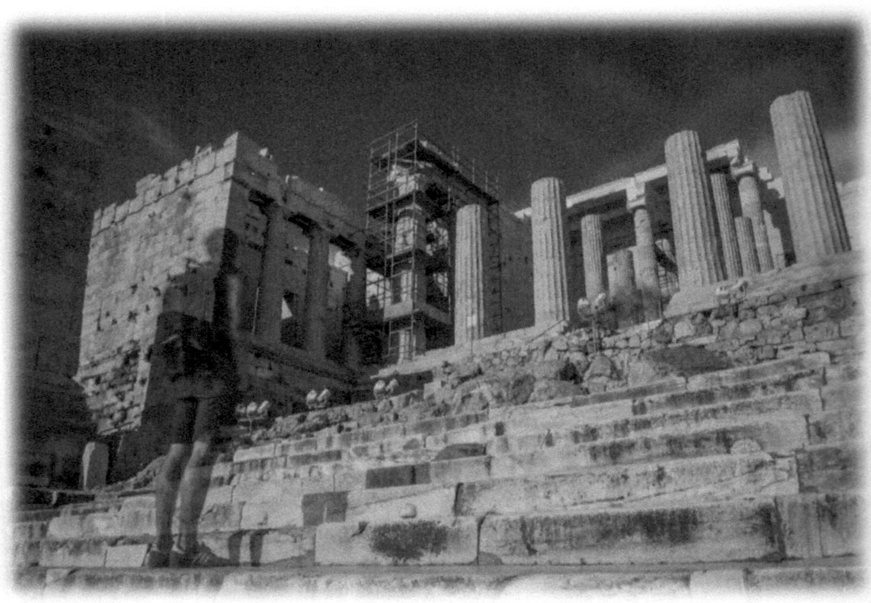

The World's New Wonders

Yes yes! Come!
See the world's new wonders
That we have built
	We, the "liberated" slaves
Who chose our bonds
Of burning technology or cold codices

You can smell the world's new wonders
The rank slaughterhouses
	Dripping with the blood of man, of beast
Who's killing floors are adorned with illimitable corpses
Like the fleshy jewels on the throne of hell

Come and feel the world's new wonders
The heavy oil sand beds
	Behold! Man has learned to drown the very sea!
Its witnesses like a million poisoned cultists
Belly up and clammy with egotistical slime

Come and taste the world's new wonders!
The dark satanic mills
	Industrial churnings to gut the golden green fields
With what efficiency they manufacture the physical!
So the spirit may become pacified and wither
As the rivers catch flame

Come, hear the world's new silence
The gray solemn plains of crushed earth,
And beyond the wastelands of concrete
The horrible roar of atom splitting songs

Come, and feast on the world's new wonders!
Chemical crops overcoming the pesky farmers
        Our superior armies of corn
Marching from unconscious manufacture, consumes the indigenous
Bred for profit while people fall down in the dust

They say keep calm, don't fight it
Soon we will be new world wonders too
Our children a monotone, conformed monocrop
One last "grand" generation,
Our genes a communion between man and petri dish
Everything uniform
No more of the troublesome variety of nature

But be weary
For the world's last wonder will be an auto-holocaust
Not a war of honorable men for democracies or freedoms
But a like a mindless black hole of morality
A vicious struggle for the last few drops of cool glacial water,
For the last trembling sight of an open horizon,
The last breath of moist forest air and
Taste of tart wild berry

I Left Scars on All My Bodies

Body made of cataclysmic happening
Made of free skin — made of calm death
Skybox compost formation grows
On the nick of the nurse log

You have to leave the mountain behind
Blood is water, is ice

Tell me how you made it through the winter
    And not long to linger
Before your give your body back

Freeze-thaw dialectics, storm weathering semiotics
Mountains dropping seeds of sky
Sky scarring out the mountains

Watershed net
Coils in the deep black

Springs back

Twenty Billion Eyes, One Heart

You don't love me that way, she tells me
In the letter it sounds like rain
Falling in fields of ash

It sounds like a world dying calmly
As if we could kill a world calmly
As if love was a material problem that could
Simply be burned away

As if love wasn't the meaning behind
The poisoned lips of the dying

She knows like she knows god
Like she knows fear
"You don't love me that way"
The way she thinks love is
      But I don't blame her

The love that they sell on T.V. and
Teach little girls at church
Smelling sterile, like unblemished bodies and fresh packaging
Zip tie romances

"Most of the time it's easy to do"
She says about love
Like it comes from an ikea storeroom
With a little set of wrenches

With a bible that says:
This is how you put
Your love together
Every time (In every language)

Nowadays people love like industrial processes
Love is best when it is made fastest
Made cheapest
Made easiest, and imported
Get up and move, don't deal with the mess

As if you don't have to give up everything for love
As if it doesn't take sorrow and suffering,
As if its value wasn't based upon it
But dark for light
Everything balances

    "See you around" she says
And she's righteous, inflammable
I can see her energy in the eyes of everyone else, realized
I had loved her for everyone in her eyes
And like the water rushing through her skin,
That our energy goes on and on in gardens of love
Rising up in hearts of mud and
Minds of flowers forever

In a dream she kneels in a dusty furrow
Her little hands outstretched, holding a match
One trying to block the wind, the other trying to burn
But love is not a field you can just burn away
Love lays in the soil, like a silver cross in a field of ashes
Even when it's buried in mud, it's still there

Love is not of this dimension, it is extra-dimensional
Dragging our bodies together
Like supermassive stars impacting
Spewing debris into abyss
Distorting time as we know it
Until matter doesn't matter
    Our love creating new verses

Maya Moon Dance (Even Buddhas Need a Mother)

Gave birth to silent night
Holy, free gift of life made branded and ragged
Smudged human body — seen through colored morality yet
    The rules of man
Have no influence on the virgin moon

In its staggering born suchness floating unbounded
    Moving like a free mother
Wildsky eyes, unpossessable

Young Marys and Mayas wane pale cast,
Wax pure — coming new
Dancing through stretched skin and renewing blood
Shedding earthly expectations of keeping time
    The body won't stay, continues through
In birth, beyond birth

Some crusty fat heads
Slicing shadow whores and light mothers like
Material body contradicts heavenly body?

Lonely poverty of earth man in whole moon-sky,
Mistaken separation of holy heaven spirit/ruined dump body
(Dis)appears in a splash

All I Could Do

When I saw you standing there
Feeling alone
I couldn't help it
I wanted to share the secret with you

To whisper to you:
"Disenfranchised angel,
Your breaking is from the weight
Of all the things society said"

I don't want to scare you
But I'm compelled to tell you
To turn your faucet on high
And let it out full

That you can't fall
That there is no ground
And you're flawless in your crashing forms
In this falling-blooming
World of truth in trash

It was all I could do
To hold back the tears
Seeing the quiver in your eyes
Skull chattering with all the mortal fears,
The uncertainties of space-time and meaning

All I could do was offer a smile,
Hope it would stick in your teeth

Twinkle with my void at your cosmic feet and
Show that underneath it all
It is the same for me

I will try not to shake, while I hold up my mirror
So yours reflects clearly

And together, our twin faced mirrors
Can hold no place for fear

That we may fall in love in this moment
And walk each other home as idols explode

Human Sky Body

Going for self-challenge
Human limit?
        Mother of waters' summit imaginary
Cloud spot where soul leaks sky

The body lives as it dies
Self-meaning?
        Young men with empty stomachs, strong legs
Rising with the mountain until only breath and water
Not just breath and water at all

At camp, fill the pot with snow
Melt enough to eat and drink
        Stove burning in heavy wind
Gas spewing, heat losing
Flame still burning through it

Spill the pot as it reaches boil
Cut a shelf for temporary shelter
Pound in a picket to guy the tent

Smile as the storm rolls in
Lay down on a leaky pad and catch a wink
Between gusts

Don't read the Diamond Sutra
Just sleep before the tent is blown away!

Weather breaks in the afternoon
        Cloud windows in the mind
But that was our bid, and there's
No time to boil water for a summit push or
Practice self-arrest
Only to bow gratefully to Floating Mountain

Thundering Mountain, Drowning Mountain
Lets us break camp and
Take our soft bodies down from the ancient ice river

Down, past squeakin' marmots and pretty girls
Down, down, down on the path I had wanted to burn
Down with our bodies in a funeral pyre by the bay
        Down to Rain City
Where Toby is napping on a pile of lifejackets
In the Green Lake boathouse

Going Home

Remember before you knew?
You didn't see the borders
    You didn't see the other

You could see clearly
We just wanted to walk each other home
    If we didn't it was because we were too afraid to ask
Because we'd become enemies on accident and hurt
Each other's feelings – worked ourselves up
And wow we got going!
    We didn't know what we were doing
But we'd have to break our selves into pieces if we admitted it

Is it too late to forgive?
    To forgive each other for our home-seeking
Group-seeking, Love-seeking, truth-seeking?

If we are going to play the game of pretending
That you are you, and I am I and
We're separate like bombs and terror or
Like wealth and poverty

Let's change the moldy rules we made up
So we each at least
"Have" a place to grow in peace

Fear All the Way Down

Mechanical procession of mourners
Stuck in traffic on the highway, smelling
Burning dreams of peace, loving-kindness,
International sisterhood, brotherhood all
Subsumed into Mercedes mentality, says:
"Everyone
Get in the fucking box...
Stop squirming, man up and kill your brother!"

Built on the socially constructed competition floor
Bomb designers and business degrees
Lining up to jump into the nucleus of aggression, say
"You're not working hard enough!"

I guess you just don't understand child
We made you up to lay you down again

Alienated laborers in the global fear factory
Inputs of manipulated desire, desperation, pitted against each other
So we forget the money changers and oil games

Confused particles constituting fear system
From predator drones to exploded hospitals in our hearts

Like hell, it's burning in me too
        Fear so thick it feels like heavy slime in our lungs
So every breath we breathe
We breathe like we're fighting or running
Our minds become closed quagmires of one anxious
Thought after another, until we can't remember
What we were to begin with

Between remembering who's trying to kill us,
Who we're supposed to kill,
And the robots coming for the work
It's being pumped into us like reverse dialysis
        All swollen with fear so as far as we remember,
As far as we reflect, it's
Fear all the way down

        The people all forgot they were free, were
Told they had to step on each other's heads to keep from drowning
To get to the top?
        (A million sounds like a lot from way down there ...and it seems
        like nobody loves you)
But nowadays the top is in liquidated space where
For peace they preach war, tell us to
Hold our grudges, get your piece and
Fight the bad world!
To divide what hoodied specters are left

Sagarmāthā Moans Death

These young mountains sing
Songs of change, deliverance
Knowing even continents can shift

Temporary states break their tortured-built backs
Banks keep the dumps in debt
Keep them from developing too fast,
And only under sanctioned stability

Foreign aid can't replace local economies (let alone ecologies)
Like the justice of spines severed in the slave catcher cop cars
Locked and raped in systematic destructions
Worked and wasted in dense prisons

But Freddie's death is not annihilation
Only the building of potential energy, for
Sagarmāthā moans death in an international tongue
     The quaking release of old tensions
Power and suffering
Factioned extraction and labor exploitation
From locked to breaking
Open ground shaking Kathmandu to Baltimore

The misery of death so overwhelming that
It strips the land of all its familiarities
Temples crumble, plutocracies and oligarchies
Shucked of their superficial husk of pleasure, leaving
The opportunity for beautiful democracies,
World community, global unity through disenchanted internality
Freedom from fear —of death certain and righteous
     No solid ground
Illusions of bodily certainty, national sovereignty to be held by
With quaking release of globalized forces
Energy moves towards equilibrium

Soggy Bus Sutra

For Thich Nhat Hanh (for all of us)

Soaking through day, through night
Pine scented world bodies wake
To celebrate liquid eyes and
Fusion flecks
Ten billion pairs of feet on the lotus rug
Made of molten rock

Fraying into toes
Divinations in the cream, bitter
Hot brew in the belly
    Hang clothes on the rest

Splash to the stop
Feet rolling in the drink, droplets
Rolling back to puddles
Through the sewers mixing

Rolling soggy bus melting glaciers
Nearing the stop
    Collective human problem
Down the road away from individual states

Forde wheel rut rivers, hydroplaning
Nightmare of separation, searching strip malls for
Dollar store bibles written by empires
Old sutras translated by sexists and racists probably

But us at the stop
We're all glad to see the dogsangha, livingwet, world dripping in
Glowing miracle of happening, together for us: Bus
    Bounding past private-coffin mentalities
Lay down, give up and
Pant in the puddles

Open to togetherness

Morning light and wet footsteps on the floor
Faces refracted in the journey
All of us accidentally meditating about "love"
        And where to get off?
Lulled by the motion

Beautiful soft girls get on the bus
Rings in their noses
Radiant star-jewels in their heads
The miracle of breath in their throat
        Wondering Where, Why their fathers went?
So they just keep riding the bus around
Trying to find a museum which will light them properly

When they get off their silhouettes
Look nothing like byzantine portraits
More like trampled beds of flowers,
Would grow into gardens if they didn't get stomped on or
Weren't tricked into trying to be a fixed image

        In the nick of time
Thay gets on the bus,
Sits down and starts talking to a homeless guy
They both left their spiritual egos at home

We joke about trying to stay dry, how
The rain doesn't get under our skin
        We get some funny looks
And just like this he's gotta go
Gives me his bus transfer and
Puts his brain on top
Like a biodegradable paperweight

Rain never came never left

Crusty Messiahs

For Revolutionaries

Jesus, your bloody ribs look like weeping forests
Caught on the structure of corrupted civilization
Loving us patiently
Giving us breath while we cut them down
     Who made you up into a freaky statue and
Locked you in the king's church?

Even death prays with his hands clasped
     But for what does he ask?
His hands look like your ribs Jesus
Begging for love and life
Pure from the free mother
Revolution against the old father

Who painted you white and
Added all those moneyed rules,
Said conversion was more sacred than life and
Put prayer over practice?

But Jesus,
I see your gnostic core
Your human loving ribs
     Your ribs are the same ribs
In the chest of Gautama,
Mohammad, and Krishna

These are just names
Not the oscillating breath of the omniscient heart-mind
Which knows beyond the intellect, sees
Beyond temporary perspective

All of the hearts are beating in syncopated rhythm
To be amplified and diversified

    Already to be woken
To play your ribs with our neighbors
So that our neighborhood earth
Our supranational community
Sounds like a marimba band
At a wedding ringed in blooming rhododendrons

Everyone dancing with hands clasped,
Swaying bones singing harmonies of love
That will go on echoing in the rock of ages
Solid, silent vibrating notes
Inspiring successive resonance

Jesus,
We let you get crusty so
I'm going to give you a bath
    To wash off all the words they wrote on your face
So we can see the mystical glint in your eyes

Non-Dual Gospel of the Mind-Body
From the Gospel of Mary

...Will matter then be destroyed or not?
The savior said
All Nature, all formations, all creatures exist
In and with one another
And they will be resolved again into their own roots

The inner lamp has been hidden
Transcendent opportunity womb—relaxed mind miracle
World mother, the free thriving almah
    Her subjugated forests
Silenced in the temples, in the forum
Market-centric value doesn't count the home

How can economies in spite of ecologies?
What can really be owned?
Only temporarily

Dying men (destructive) trying to control the transdimensional
Worlds of seeds, beyond motherhood, re/production
Towards the nature of god, the creativity in chaos

Matter gave birth to a passion that has no equal

And all the bodily fears of passion and loss
Of attached fragility
Of shortsighted separateness
Birthed stillborn Impure–Pure dichotomies
Virginity mis/conception and boys afraid of blood

The chastity belt illusion clapped on the mind of young
Girls whether Christian, Hindu or Muslim
Stabbing at the divine whole
Until a hole was all that was left

...But if the Savior made her worthy,
Who are you indeed to reject her?
Surely the Savior knows her very well.

...Desire said, I did not see you descending,
But now I see you ascending.
Why do you lie since you belong to me?
The soul answered and said, I saw you.
You did not see me nor recognize me.
I served you as a garment and you did not know me.

The Home of Being

The oceans are calling to corporeal Selfs
Hydrogen hierarchies from Starbellies to Riverhearts to Dreameyes
Skyscraper moneychangers bleed greed oil
When they stand against the love lugey of God

The oceans are rising
And the children are mixing water with dust
Making clots of mud
For who are the borders of nations?

How to count droplets, faces, species?
All of the beings, meanings, dreamings
Dancing through myriad hand gestures of the oceans
Waterflesh breathes Waterbreath
Lives Waterlight

The Oceans are rising
That the waves will rend the cities to sand

For when the water comes out flame
The farmers fall to their knees
Screaming through dry throats

Then they rise like the water

Standing in buzzing waves of bees
Surging like the hearts of horses
In the bodies of apes

These are Our Eyes

These are our sinking rafts
Our intellectual dogmas
These are the things that we tie our asses to while
We breathe

These are our bodies
These are our chains
The forms of our words

Expectations,
And the physically-trained experience of a solitary body

But if we close our eyes
We are free
        To accept the flux
To be the winds of chaotic peace
To rust iron cages

If we close our eyes
We are free
        No darkness of separation
No polemics of the body

If we close our eyes
We are free
        To ask us, about ourselves
What came first
The question or the questioner?

If we close our eyes
We are free
        To find the child hiding behind the jade
To say the word more over and over and over
Until it loses its meaning

So it sounds ridiculous
Like someone crying
Whose laugh sounds like someone crying
        And we can see without differentiating illusions
That we are.
That we are all we need

If we close our eyes
We are free
Again a part of the dynamic universe
            Didn't your momma tell you?
Object permanence isn't just a survival skill
It's an enlightenment skill

The world is your heart beating, crashing, changing
In infinite rhythms,
Don't try to keep it in
Your bone prison

When our eyes are closed
When we forget that someone ever told us that
Our eyes exist

We are free to see with all the eyes to ever exist
To see that fear is a position we take
To knead joy, with the breath, back into the spirit
To say to all the beings and nonbeings:
"Regardless of whether I understand you, I love you."

Come Down from the Mountain and Love!

Eventually you'll have to come down from your mountain
And dump everything you built like
A pile of charred symbols

Don't worry
There will be other mountains, rivers
    Do they ever end?
Other fermented feels about gods walking with you
Walking through you

Now, be calm as you come down
    Hear the glaciers, feel the fires
Churn with you
Flow in you

Go you!
Go down!
Down from ideas about motorcycle masculinity and perfect vaginas
Down from anxieties about your classmates
    Kiss their cheeks and bless them on their way
You didn't know this would be the last time
But everybody's got a body to lose

Share a laugh as you go down
Laugh at your self
Let it echo off the sky

Don't get stuck up there!
Cause your body won't last
You can't keep the house clean
You're going to break the glass

See as far as there is to be
Then come down and join the sea

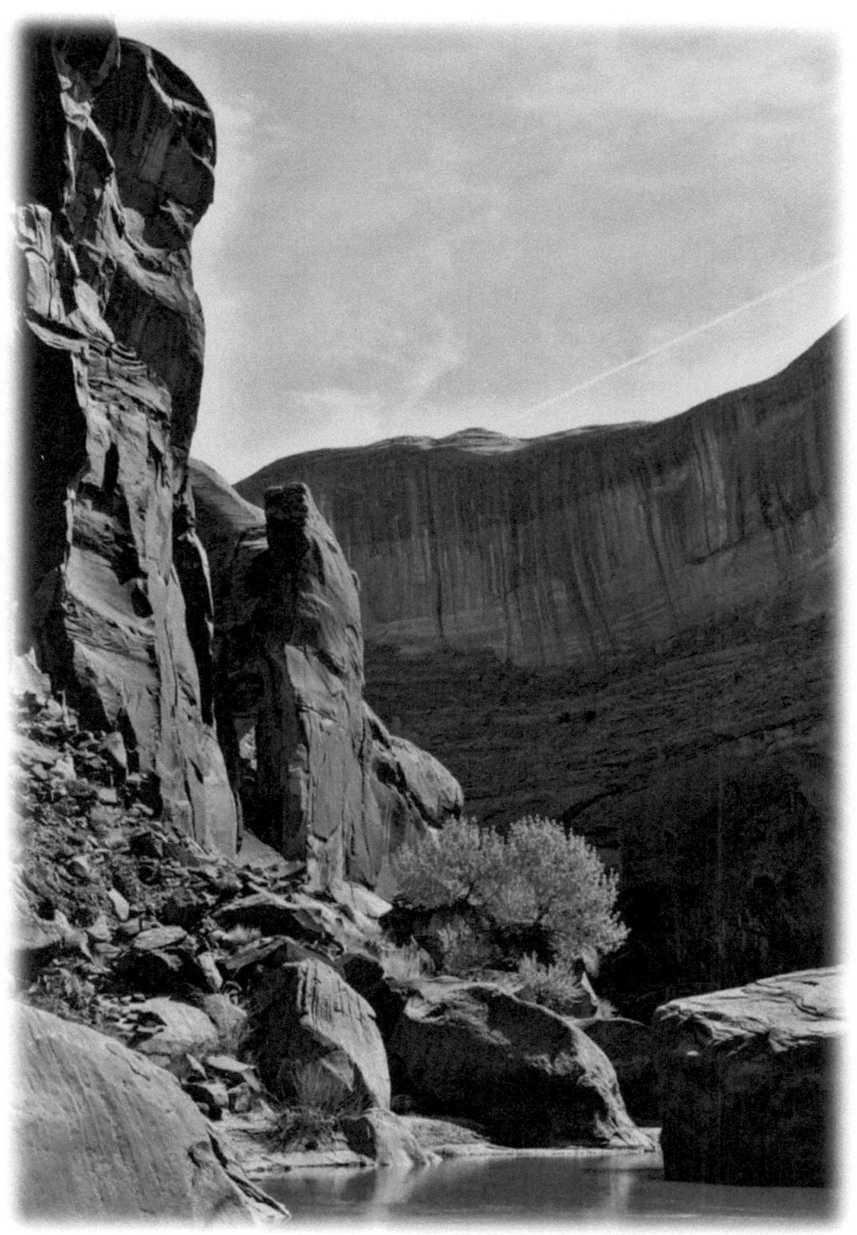

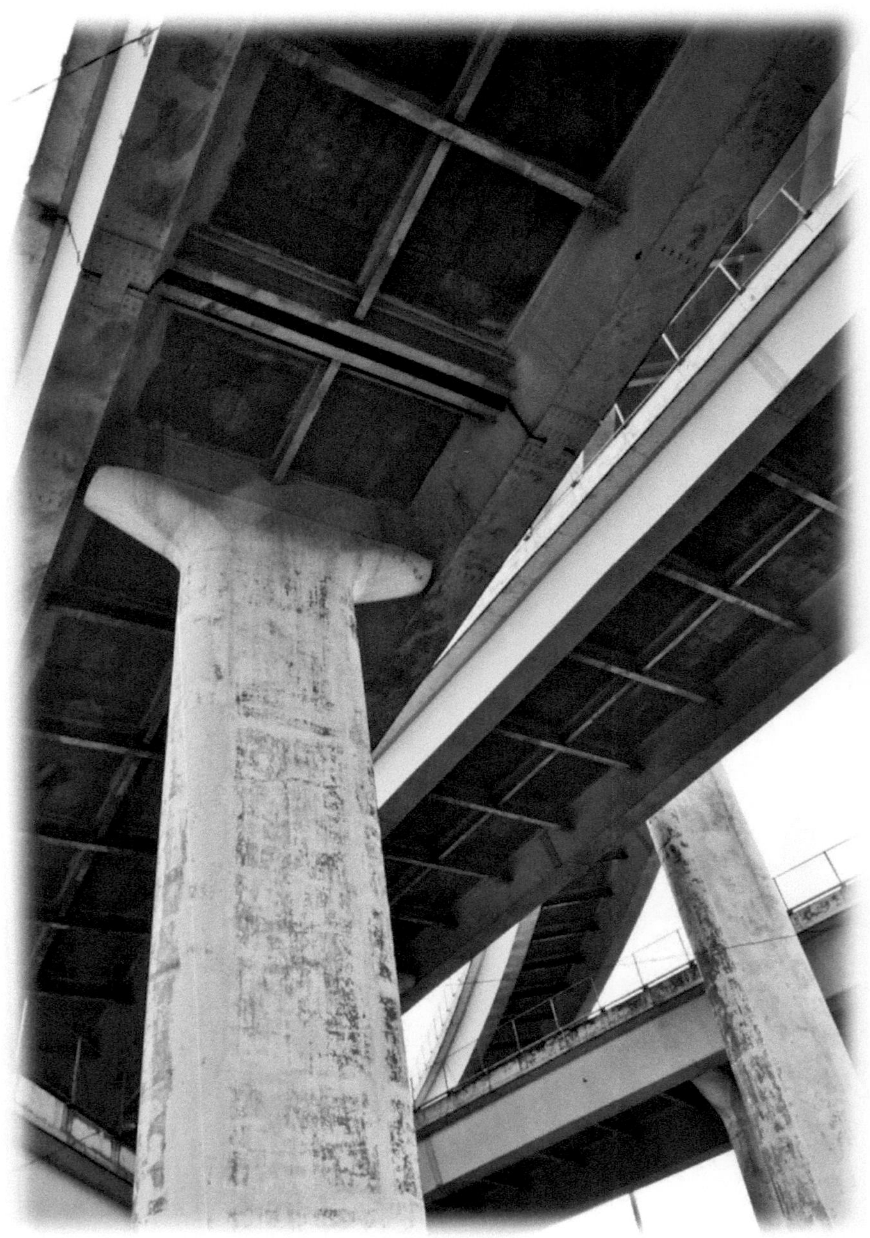

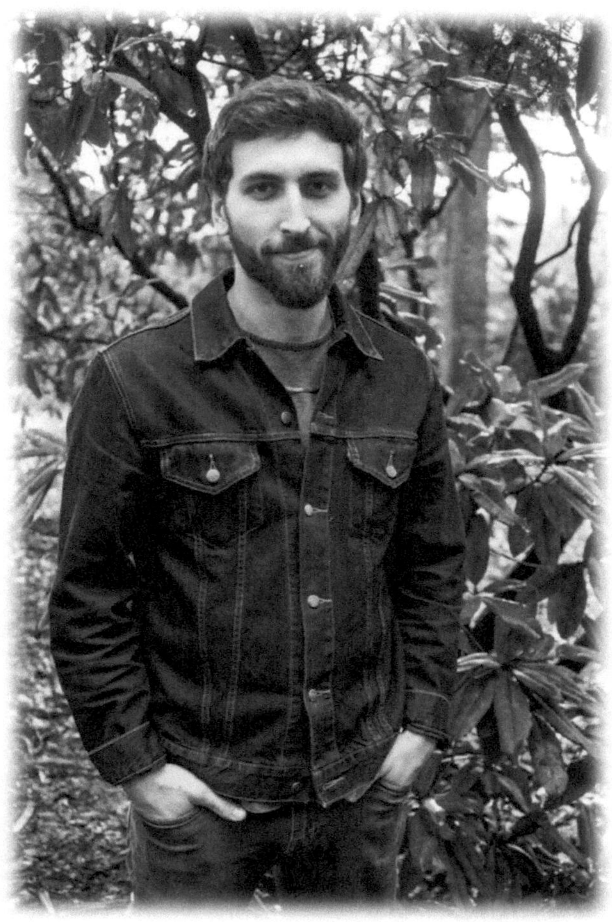

Cody Owen was born September 19, 1992 and raised in Portland, Oregon. Growing up in the pacific northwest, meeting many kind people, and visiting the ocean, mountains and high desert, he was inspired by the interdependence of human and natural systems. Sometimes working as a mountain guide, Cody studies society and social movements, political-economy, philosophy, religion, Zen, digging holes in the ground, and himself, among other natural phenomena. He is a forgivable sinner and loves whatever gets you out of bed in the morning, but especially compassion, forgiveness, creativity, dreams and the unity of living things.

Printed by Libri Plureos GmbH in Hamburg,
Germany